Healing in the Presence of the Lord

Workbook

Natalie Degraffinreaidt

Healing in the Presence of the Lord - Workbook

Copyright © 2018 by Natalie Degraffinreaidt

All rights reserved. No part of this book may be reproduced or transmitted in any form or by any means without written permission of the author.

King James Version, Scripture quotations marked "KJV" are taken from the Holy Bible, King James Version (Public Domain).

ISBN 978-1-947741-25-6

Workbook published by:

Kingdom Publishing LLC
Odenton, MD 21113

First printed in the U.S.A.

Table of Contents

Introduction 1

Chapter 1 - Childhood Crisis 3

Chapter 2 - Teenage Pregnancy 5

Chapter 3 - Self-Identity Crisis 9

Chapter 4 - The Idle Mind is the Devil's Playground 11

Chapter 5 - Fear 15

Chapter 6 - Drugs 17

Chapter 7 - Marriage 21

Chapter 8 - Being a Wife 25

Chapter 9 - The Rotten Wife 27

Chapter 10 - The Battered Wife 31

Chapter 11 - Walking into My Healing 35

Chapter 12 - Forgiving 37

Chapter 13 - Deliverance 41

Chapter 14 - Connections 43

Chapter 15 - Obedience 47

In Closing 49

Introduction

This workbook has been created to help you through your own healing process; whether it be from emotional, physical, spiritual, sexual, verbal or drug abuse. I pray my book gives you deep revelation of areas in your life you may need healing in, so that you can move forward to be the best you and walk into your destiny. In order to complete this workbook, you must read the book and follow along as you meditate on each chapter of the book.

Be sure to take your time as you read through the book and allow it to truly minister to you. This book will take you on a journey to face the truth about yourself and the things that are buried deep within you that are keeping you from your healing. You must be ready to receive your healing and face the truth. The truth may feel devastating at the present time but ultimately will set you free. Begin to prepare your heart and mind now for this journey.

Taking the healing journey is never easy, but it's very rewarding. I promise you from my own experiences, the pain from facing the truth has been hard, but has truly been liberating. I used to numb the truth within in order to face myself day to day. I pray by the end of this workbook you will be able to face things that you thought never impacted your life; the things that have formed you into the person opposite of what God has called you to be in Him. Now let the journey begin! Below is a prayer for you to recite before you begin your healing journey.

Prayer for Healing

Lord, I (fill in your name) come to you asking for your guidance on this healing journey. I don't know how this process will turn out, but I know that I am going to need your strength. Please allow me to acknowledge the truth of any pain that has kept me from living the life I know am intended to live. Lord, help me to be honest with myself and not to be in denial of my past or present pain from the people around me.

Father, please clean up any deep rooted wounds within me that need to be cleaned up. I thank you Lord for being with me and loving me so much that you led me to this point in my life so that I can receive your healing. I'm choosing to take this step so I can experience the freedom in you because of your unfailing love towards me. In Jesus name, Amen.

Chapter 1

Childhood Crisis

After reading this chapter of the book, think about your own life and answer the following questions below. Please be honest with yourself. I can't stress enough the importance of your honesty towards yourself. Being honest with yourself, will help you grow to the next level on this journey so that you can receive your healing.

Scripture: **Proverbs: 22:6** (KJV)
"Train up a child in the way he should go: and when he is old, he will not depart from it."

1. How was your childhood?

2. What type of seeds (words or actions) did your parent(s) or other people plant inside of you as a child?

3.   Did you experience any type of abuse as a child? Example...Sexual, drug, emotional, physical, spiritual or mental? If, so how do you believe this abuse impacted your life?

4.   What type of feelings sprung up in you by tapping into this area of your life?

5.   Take a moment to write down the name of each person that abused you matching the type of abuse with the name. For example...

    Joe sexually abused me.

    Nick emotionally abused me.

Chapter 2

Teenage Pregnancy

Everyone may not be able to relate to this chapter, but some probably can. This chapter of my book is dealing with me becoming pregnant as a teenager and the emotions that came along with that, as well as the different experiences I encountered through this process including physical abuse. If you have experienced any of the things mentioned in this chapter meditate on them and answer the questions below.

1.   How did you feel about yourself as a teenager?

2.   Were you confident in yourself or were you an attention seeker?

3. What age did you lose your virginity?

4. Did you get pregnant as a teenager, if so what type of emotions did it cause you to have?

5. What type of coping strategies did you use to help cope with any negative feelings or emotions?

6. Did you suffer from low self-esteem? If so how did this affect your life as a teenager and young adult?

7. Have you been running from the truth of things that have transpired in your life?

8. If so, why are you in fear of facing the truth?

9. Write down some things you could relate to in this chapter! Take some time to truly reflect and write down your own experiences!

Chapter 3

Self-Identity Crisis

Scripture: Galatians 6:7-8
"Do not be deceived: God cannot be mocked. A man reaps what he sows. Whoever sows to please their flesh will reap destruction; whoever sows to please the spirit, from the spirit will reap eternal life."

1. Have you lost your true identity?

2. If so, what kind of things or experiences has formed you into the person you are today?

3. What type of things or people contaminated you?

4.   Have you ever had feelings for or were involved with someone of the same sex?

5.   What do you think drove you to mess with a person of the same sex as you?

6.   Do you see how your crises, from childhood up to now have shaped your identity? Remember, you are not your past and don't allow it to continue to define you.

7.   Reflect on this chapter and the questions above. What have you learned about yourself so far?

Chapter 4

The Idle Mind is the Devil's Playground

Scripture: 2 Corinthians 10:3-6

"For though we live in the world, we do not wage war as the world does. The weapons, we fight with are not weapons of the world. On the contrary, they have divine power to demolish strongholds. We demolish arguments and every pretension that sets itself up against the knowledge of God, and we take captive every thought to make it obedient to Christ. And we will be ready to punish every act of disobedience, once your obedience is complete."

1. What type of thoughts have you allowed to control your life?

2. How are you occupying your mind?

3. What does your day consist of you doing?

4. What are your eyes fixed on? Remember the eyes are the gateway to the heart.

5. What type of seeds are you planting for growth on a daily basis, negative or positive?

6. What fleshly desires are you still feeding?

7. What type of thoughts have placed you in prison in your mind?

8. What will it take to get out of the prison of your mind?

9.   Reflection of this chapter. Write down some things you have learned about yourself and how things could change for your life! What areas have you learned that you need healing in?

Remember: Don't allow your past failures to determine your future; we need to go through the struggle in order to be successful. If we never go through the struggle how would we learn to appreciate the life Christ has given us. He removed us from the age of darkness. No matter how long it may seem, please understand that God has not forgotten about you. Hold on to his promises and your reward will be great. Work hard to be who Christ called you to be; walking in His image and not the image man has of you. God created us to have life more abundantly in Him; outside of Him is a life of hell. Don't be blinded by the things of this world that keep us locked away for so long, but stand firm by the renewing of your mind.

Scripture: *"Therefore, remember that formerly you who are Gentiles by birth and called 'uncircumcised' by those who call themselves 'the circumcision'(Which is done in the body by human hands)remember at that time you were separate from Christ, excluded from citizenship in Israel and foreigners to the covenants of the promise, without hope and without God in the world."*

Chapter 5

Fear

Fear of other people's opinion of me caused me to wrap myself up inside of a box unable to breathe. I feared the unknown reaction of people, that is, if they would accept me after finding out the truth. Fear kept me in a place where life was being sucked out of me. I could no longer breathe, just going through life as a zombie.

1. Define what fear means to you.

2. Has fear crippled you in life?

3. How has fear affected your life?

4.   Has fear controlled your life? If so, in what type of way?

5.   What type of pain have you afflicted on other people because of your secrets buried within?

6.   What type of steps can you take to overcome your fears?

7.   Reflection: As you review this chapter in the book and look over your questions, what have you learned about yourself in this chapter? Take the necessary time to reflect on this question.

Chapter 6

Drugs

I took drugs to suppress the real me. I no longer knew who I was. I allowed everything to contaminate me on this journey. I used drugs to help me cope with everyday life. I did not like my life and was not pleased with where it was heading. I was controlled by my pain and allowed it to dictate my actions. I didn't want to feel the pain any longer, so I buried it by taking different types of prescription pills. I took every pain medication possible to numb my pain.

My heart was aching beyond measure; I just didn't want to feel the pain any longer. I just wanted to feel good. The drugs were my escape plan. They helped me feel good and took my mind off the issues in those moments. My self-destructive behavior caused me more damage than I fully understood at the time.

1. Have you been introduced to drugs?

    ■1b. If so, what type of drugs have you been introduced to?

2. How long have you been on these drugs?

3. Why do you feel like you are using these drugs?

4. Have you been running from yourself? If so, why are you scared to face yourself?

5. Why are you suppressing the true you? You are beautifully and wonderfully made by our master above!

6. What don't you like about yourself that you need to change?

■6b. How are you going to work on changing these things about yourself?

7. What step are you going to take in order for you to stop using drugs?

8. Reflection: What have you learned about yourself after reading this chapter and reviewing the questions? Please take a moment and think!! Write your reflection answer below. Remember, it is best to face the truth about yourself and be set free from anything that is causing you to harm yourself! Understand, we can cause more harm to ourselves by placing drugs into our system and running from our true self! Don't run any longer; walk into your deliverance to see the true you! The Lord will turn your ashes to beauty in due season.

Chapter 7

Marriage

At 25, I married the father of my children. We were still kids ourselves, unstable and starting a family of our own. We didn't even know the true meaning of marriage. We only went by what we seen and what we were brought up around. We both were brought up inside of broken homes, being broken ourselves and having nothing to offer one another. The love we knew, was love based on our own standards not based on the true foundation of God.

1. Are you married?

■ 1b. How old were you when you got married?

2. Were you ready for marriage or were you pressured into marriage due to people's opinion of you?

3. Did you bring baggage into your marriage?

- 3b. What type of baggage did you bring into your marriage?

4. Do you understand the true meaning of marriage?

5. How do you define marriage and love in a marriage?

6. How has getting married prematurely affected your decisions as a parent and spouse?

7. Do you have any stability in your life?

8. Did you get married to fill a void in your heart?

9. What type of struggles are you experiencing in your marriage, due to your lack of stability and financial limitation?

10. Reflection: Take a moment and reflect on this chapter and these questions. Please be honest with yourself. What have you learned about yourself in this chapter?

Chapter 8

Being a Wife

It was so hard for me to manage my home properly as a wife and mother. I was suffering from so much pain and I needed deliverance from myself so that I could become the best wife God had called me to be. I needed to heal so I could continue on this journey. I was under so much pressure as a wife and young mother. I was trying to run the household, manage the children and make sure I stayed committed to my church as well. I don't even know how I managed to do all the things I did. There were so many things on my plate, it had to have been the Lord's mercy that got me through. I give all the glory to the Lord!

1. How does it feel being a wife?

2. Is it hard for you to manage your home properly as a wife?

3.	What type of pain and pressure are you under?

4.	What is your perception of family and the church?

> ■ 4b. Do you believe the church comes before your family?

5.	Do you believe you are in control of everything including your husband?

6.	What type of changes would you like to see happen in your life?

7.	Reflection: Think about this chapter and these questions. Take a moment to reflect on this chapter and write below what you've learned about yourself. Take the time needed to really reflect on your response.

Chapter 9

The Rotten Wife

Something rotten leaves a bad odor. It stinks and the longer you leave that rotten thing around the stronger the smell becomes. That's how I was as a wife in the beginning of my marriage. All the junk I had buried within me left a bad odor. My unpleasant scent wasn't what people wanted to smell. I had a bad attitude, an unforgiving heart, and selfish ambitions. I was full of anger, a backbiter, murderer, and a liar. I was manipulative, controlling, jealous, bitter, and the list goes on. Everything about me was nasty. Even I didn't realize how nasty I really was back then.

1. What does it mean to be a rotten wife to you?

2. Do you believe you are a rotten wife?

3. Are you harboring unforgiveness in your heart towards your husband?

4. Do you manipulate situations and lie? Are you full of anger and do you walk around with a bad attitude and try to control everything around you?

- 4b. If you answered yes to the question above, what emotion/s are driving you to be the way you are?

5. Do you encourage your husband or discourage him with your words and actions?

6. Do you manipulate your husband to catch him in his lies?

7. How do you think your actions make your husband feel as a man?

8.   Do you communicate with your husband about your feelings and ask him about his feelings?

9.   Do you make decisions based off of your feelings or do you use sound judgement?

10.   Is there anything in your life you have been keeping from your husband?

   ■ 10b. Is there anything you need to tell your husband about you?

11.   If so write it out and write out ways you could begin to trust your husband with your heart.

12.   Do you believe you are working with your husband or against him?

13.   Reflection: After reading this chapter and reviewing the questions, think about your own life. What have you learned about yourself and what can you do to become better in those areas? Take a moment to answer the question below.

Chapter 10

The Battered Wife

A woman that has been battered is very fragile and easily broken. She may have been misused by many, physically, mentally, emotionally, and verbally through abusive relationships. This type of woman is a very delicate package and needs to be handled with special care. She should have a warning sign on her that states "fragile item inside, easily damaged." Any time she is treated carelessly that sign is disregarded, and she becomes damaged.

When battered person syndrome (BPS) manifests as PTSD, it consists of the following symptoms: (a) re-experiencing the battering as if it were recurring even when it is not, (b) attempts to avoid the psychological impact of battering by avoiding activities, people, and emotions, (c) hyperarousal or hypervigilance, (d) disrupted interpersonal relationships, (e) body image distortion or other somatic concerns, and (f) sexuality and intimacy issues.

Additionally, repeated cycles of violence and reconciliation can result in the following beliefs and attitudes.

❶ The abused think that the violence was his or her fault.

❷ The abused has an inability to place the responsibility for the violence elsewhere.

❸ The abused fear for her/his life, and/or, the lives of loved ones whom the abuser might or has threatened to harm (e.g., children-in-common, close relatives or friends).

❹ The abused has an irrational belief that the abuser is omnipresent and omniscient. Define by Wikipedia.

1. Have you been battered?

2. Do you suffer from the battered woman syndrome?

3. What type of abuse have you experienced in your marriage or any other relationships?

4. How did this abuse make you feel and why do you believe you tolerated such abuse?

5. Do you feel emotionally and physically inadequate? If so what type of steps could you take to break free from this feeling?

6. How do you view yourself as a woman?

7. What type of steps could you take to break out of the battered woman syndrome?

8. Are you willing to take the necessary steps to overcome this victim mentality?

9. Write down the name of the person(s) who have battered you.

■ 9b. Write down what you would like your abuser to know. Write him or her a letter, expressing yourself to him/her. Make sure you write all the pain he/she has caused you in the letter.

10. Reflection: After reading this chapter and reviewing the questions, what have you learned about yourself? Write below what you've learned. Take the time necessary to reflect on this chapter.

Chapter 11

Walking into My Healing

In order for me to walk in my healing, I had to start forgiving whoever had caused me pain in my life. This was not an easy process. All the things that I had ever covered up had to be exposed, in order for me to receive my healing. I had to forgive every person and forget about the pain buried so deep within me. God began to show my hardened heart to me. I didn't realize how hard my heart had become. I had become so accustomed to just pretending nothing mattered that I was numb to the truth. It was much easier for me to pretend everything was fine instead of facing the reality.

1. Write down the name of the people you need to forgive.

    ■ 1b. Write down what you need to forgive these people for.

2. What have you covered up that needs to be exposed, in order for you to receive your healing?

3. What negative thoughts caused you to become numb and running in circles on this journey?

4. Write a note to everyone who has hurt you and work on your forgiveness towards them. Release yourself from the pain and unhardened your heart.

5. Reflection: Take a moment and reflect on this chapter and the questions. Write below what you have learned about yourself. Take the necessary time needed to reflect on this chapter.

Chapter 12

Forgiving

There are so many mistakes that I made because of the mental state I was in. I felt so guilty about all of my actions. After I asked God for forgiveness, I learned how to forgive myself. I made sure I told my husband everything about me that he didn't know. I had to be honest with him. I never truly allowed my husband to enter my heart because of all the bad experiences I had gone through. I didn't think my husband would accept me, so I had to reveal my secrets. God was restoring everything in my life so that I could walk in my healing! By His stripes I am healed.

1.   What does forgiveness mean to you?

2.   Are you full of guilt?

3.   God forgives us constantly for our mistakes. Do you believe God forgives you?

■3b. If you answered "NO" why don't you believe God forgives you? Don't you know there is no sin too great for God to forgive you for?

4.   How can you begin to forgive yourself of your past mistakes?

5.   How can you begin to walk away from your old ways of thinking and into the way God would have you to think?

6.   What areas in your life do you need to grow and get out of your comfort zone?

7. Relationships are ruined because of miscommunication. How could you do better with communicating your true feelings to other people, in order to have healthy relationships?

8. What things do you need to confront in your own life and take complete ownership of? Many times we don't like to take ownership of the part we played in hurting other people. Take the time out to meditate on the role you played and take ownership of your own mess. This will help you begin to walk in your healing and face the truth about yourself in the process so that you can grow!

9. Reflect: Take a moment to reflect on this chapter and the questions. Take a moment to review the chapter and reflect on what you've learned about yourself. Take the necessary time you need to reflect on your answer and write it below.

Chapter 13

Deliverance

The Lord had to bring me to a place by myself, so I could become free from myself and current condition. The more I forgave and asked others for forgiveness and faced the truth, the more I became free from all of the drugs! God took away the desire for the different pills I had been using to suppress my true feelings. My desire to smoke weed and cigarettes was taken away from me too. The more I walked in the truth, the more things were coming off of me that were not of God. I was set free from every spirit that held me hostage! Those spirits had kept me in the dark for so long, I couldn't see the light. When the Lord shined His light in my life a sudden change came over me. The power of God is being manifested in my life now.

1. Define what it means to be free.

2. Do you believe you are free?

3. What type of thoughts are keeping you in bondage?

4. How have your thoughts created your reality?

5. Name some of your strongholds.

6. How can you begin to walk in your deliverance?

7. How can you take baby steps into your healing?

8. Reflection: Take a moment and think about this chapter and the questions. Reflect on the chapter and write what you learned about yourself below. Take the necessary time needed to reflect on this chapter. Remember not to deceive yourself, but be honest with yourself, in order to receive your deliverance!

Chapter 14

Connections

It is important for you to understand that who you are connected to makes a major impact on your life. For example, if you don't have your lamp plugged into the socket; when you hit the switch the light won't come on. Believe it or not that's how it is with the people in our lives. If we are connected to negative people, in return there will be no light. The only source we'll get in return is complete darkness. Remember, negativity + negativity = negative source of energy! This will drain the life out of you. Being connected to the wrong people is like dragging dead weight that slows you down. You need to break free from these type of people.

1. What type of people surround you?

2. Write down the names of the people who make a positive impact in your life.

    ■ 2b. Write down how each person has impacted your life in a positive way.

3. Write down the names of the people who make a negative impact in your life.

- 3b. Write down how each person has impacted your life in a negative way.

4. Write down the names of the people you need to disconnect yourself from.

- 4b. Why do you believe you need to disconnect from these individuals?

5. Write down the names of the people you need to stay connected too.

- 5b. Why do you believe you need to stay connected to these people?

6. Why is it important to be connected to the proper people in your life?

7. Reflection: Take a moment and reflect on this chapter and the questions. Write below what you have learned about yourself in this chapter. Remember to be honest with yourself. This is a part of your healing process.

Chapter 15

Obedience

The word of God states, *"Obedience is better than sacrifice."* Obedience is surrendering to God's plan for your life and letting go of your own will! I said, "Okay Lord, I trust you with my life; I just want to do your will!" Yet, His will didn't make sense because I couldn't understand it, so I began to do things my way…again. The Lord always made it clear what he wanted me to do; I just turned a deaf ear like I didn't hear him speaking. I have always found it difficult to be obedient. I'm not proud of this, but the truth is I'm very stubborn! My stubbornness prevented me from being obedient when I received assignments from God. I had issues with the people in the assignments. I found myself questioning God, and asking Him "Why me?!"

1.   Define obedience…

2.   Do you believe God speaks to you?

3.   What do you believe God told you to do that you refuse to complete due to the assignment?

4.   Do you trust God's plan for your life? His word states, he has plans to prosper you and give you hope for the future. Do you believe that for yourself?

5.   What is preventing you from trusting God with your life?

6.   What do you need to let go of in your life in order to follow God's plan for your life?

7.   Reflection: Think about this chapter and the questions. Reflect and write what you learned about yourself below. Remember to be honest with yourself. Your obedience to God is connected to other people in your life. Souls are connected to you. Obedience is better than sacrifice!!

In Closing

I pray you had the time to learn a lot about yourself and receive your healing. Allow this book to help you find the root of your pain and search out the truth…which lives deep within you. You are able to become the person God has designed you to be in Him. In order to become that person, you must receive your healing and be restored to your rightful place in Him. I pray this book has helped you to no longer be a victim but a survivor, taking baby steps into your healing.

I pray you start taking back power over your life that many people have stolen from you. Start by forgiving all of your abusers. I promise you, you will be liberated and free from the afflictions others have caused you. We must diligently seek God for our healing and trust him through the process. Remember, the more you hold against an individual, the more you give them power over you! It's time to get your power back!

Be honest about where you are currently in your life and where you have been traveling on your journey up to now. You will make it to your destination. You just need to begin walking in your healing and searching out the truth. I pray you begin to accept you! Don't allow your past or present pain define you any longer! You are more than a conquer in Christ! Don't condemn yourself any longer or condemn those around you! It's time to move forward and live the life you're designed to live Christ!

Take your baby steps! It's best to begin moving forward instead of not moving at all! Be of good courage! Blessings to you! I can't wait until you blossom as that beautiful rose!

www.ingramcontent.com/pod-product-compliance
Lightning Source LLC
Chambersburg PA
CBHW081356080526
44588CB00016B/2516